owning a pet
CAT

Ben Hoare

W

FRANKLIN WATTS
LONDON • SYDNEY

First published in 2005 by
Franklin Watts
96 Leonard Street
London
EC2A 4XD

Franklin Watts Australia
45–51 Huntley Street
Alexandria, NSW 2015

© Franklin Watts 2005

Series editor: Adrian Cole
Series design: Sarah Borny
Art director: Jonathan Hair
Picture researcher: Kathy Lockley
Illustrations by: Hannah Matthews

A CIP catalogue record for this book is
available from the British Library.

ISBN: 0 7496 5924 6

Dewey classification 636.8

Printed in China

The author and publisher would like to thank the following people
and cats for their contribution to the production of this book:

Nat Redfern and Anna Broke, Russell Holdsworth, Jasper and Minnie,
Noodles, Felix the cat.

Acknowledgements:
Alley Cat Productions/Alamy Images 5.
Peter Arnold/Still Pictures 27 b.
Ashmolean Museum, University of Oxford, UK/ Bridgeman Art Library London 6 t.
George Bernard/NHPA 25.
Tim Bird/Alamy Images 14 tr.
Adrian Cole 20 cl. Mary Evans Picture Library 7.
Isobel Flynn/Alamy Images 15.
D. Robert Franz/Alamy Images 26 b.
Robert Harding Picture Library 6 b.
Martin Harvey/Still Pictures 27 t. Paal Hermansen/NHPA 24.
Russell Holdsworth 21 b, 21 t, 28. Juniors Bildarchiv/Alamy Images 8 cr.
Klein/Still Pictures 4, 9 b, 9 t, 13 t, 19 t, 22 c, 22 b.
Yves Lanceau/ N.H.P.A. 16 t.
Elizabeth MacAndrew/NHPA 19 b. Charles Mistral/Alamy Images 10 b.
Ray Moller title page, 11, 17 r, 18 t. Fritz Poelking/Alamy Images 26 t.
Lynne Silver/Alamy Images 14 bl. Robert Slade/Alamy Images 18 b.
Eric Soder/NHPA 17 l. Harald Theissen/Alamy Images 29.

Contents

Pet cats

Cats make excellent pets. They are beautiful, fascinating to watch and fun to play with. Looking after a cat is not very difficult, but it is a big responsibility.

Cats are one of the most popular types of pet. There are nearly 400 million pet cats all over the world! They come in a wide variety of colours and characters, ranging from elegant pedigrees to cheeky, mixed-breed moggies. Unlike their wild relations – for example, lions, tigers and leopards – domestic cats make loveable companions. What's more, their independent and charismatic natures can provide hours of entertainment.

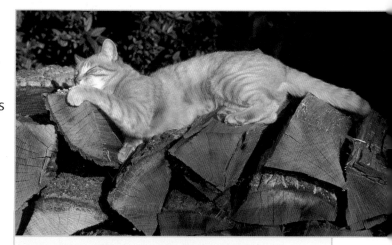

Cats love to relax, especially in the sun. They are more independent than many pets, but they still need care from their owners.

DUTY OF CARE

RSPCA International has outlined five basic rights that should be granted to all pets:

- **Freedom from hunger and thirst**
- **Freedom from discomfort**
- **Freedom from pain, injury and disease**
- **Freedom to express normal behaviour**
- **Freedom from fear and distress**

What a cat needs

Owning a cat is a major commitment because it depends on you for all its needs. These include food, medicine, a safe place to live and visits to the vet. It will also want plenty of attention, especially if it is a kitten. Cats don't have to be walked like dogs, but they do need exercise. Take time to decide if you and your parents have enough time and patience to look after a cat.

"Remember that cats normally live for more than 12 years!"

ARE YOU READY FOR A CAT?

Every year thousands of cats are abandoned because people no longer want them. So make sure you're certain that a cat is the right pet for you. Ask yourself the following questions – you should be able to answer 'yes' to each one.

- Is your whole family keen to have a cat?

- Can your family afford to pay for food, vet bills and other costs such as cattery fees when you go on holiday?

- Do you have time each day to play with, cuddle and groom a cat?

- Will you be happy if your pet sometimes doesn't want to play when you do?

- Is your home a safe place for a cat to live, with a secure area outside to explore, well away from busy roads?

- Will young children or other pets in your household get on well with a cat?

- Do you know someone who could look after your cat when you are away on holiday?

Cats can usually learn to get along with other pets, if they're introduced at an early age. They may even become best friends!

OBEYING THE LAW

There are laws protecting cats, as with most animals that we keep as pets. It is illegal to harm cats in any way. Animal welfare officers from the local council have the power to prosecute cat owners who mistreat their pets. They can impose heavy fines as punishment and may confiscate the animals.

Cats and people

Humans have lived with cats for thousands of years. In the past, some civilisations worshipped cats, while others feared or persecuted them.

Ancient alley cats

Archaeologists have found cat bones dating back 6,000–8,500 years among the ruins of ancient towns in Israel, Syria and Pakistan. It is unlikely that these bones belonged to pets. Instead, the cats probably roamed the streets as wild animals. These 'alley cats' must have been popular because they caught the rats and mice that raided grain and other food stores.

Egyptian idols

The first people to tame cats were the Ancient Egyptians, about 3,000–4,000 years ago. Cats were extremely important in Ancient Egyptian society. When they died, their owners would shave off their eyebrows as a sign of respect. The bodies of dead cats were preserved by mummification and buried together in vast tombs. One tomb explored in the nineteenth century contained 300,000 mummified cats. The Ancient Egyptians worshipped several cat gods, including Sekhmet and Bastet, which had cats' faces and women's bodies. The famous Great Sphinx (left) that still stands at Giza, near Cairo, is a carved stone monument with the head of a pharaoh and the body of a big cat – the lion.

"In some parts of the world, black cats are still thought to be bad omens – but in the UK they are symbols of good luck!"

In medieval Europe, priests declared that cats had magical powers and worked for witches or the devil. They were accused of being lazy and greedy, and many were beaten or killed.

East and west

During the Roman Empire (510 BCE–476 CE), cats spread throughout Europe. They were highly valued for their mouse-catching skills and soon became a familiar sight. Merchants also took cats to Asia and the Far East, where they were popular in palaces and monasteries. In China and Japan, cats became a symbol of wellbeing. Oriental cats remained slender, with long legs and delicate heads, like their Egyptian ancestors. In the West, however, they gradually developed the stockier build and rounder heads of most common breeds today. European settlers took domestic cats with them to North America in the 1600s and 1700s and to Australia in the 1800s.

BEST OF BREEDS

In 1871, the first ever cat show took place in London. It triggered an interest in different coat types and colours, and people began to develop the first cat breeds. Since then, cats have been bred for all sorts of characteristics. Today, there are nearly 50 official domestic cat breeds in the world.

Types of cat

Cats come in many colours, shapes and sizes. Purebreds, or pedigrees, always share distinctive characteristics, though the colour of their eyes and coat may vary.

A SELECTION OF CAT BREEDS

Abyssinian

American Bobtail

Balinese

Birman

Bombay

British Shorthair

Burmese

Chartreux

Colourpoint Shorthair

Cornish Rex

Javanese

Manx

Oriental

Siberian

Somali

Sphynx

SIAMESE

The elegant Siamese originates from Thailand (formerly known as Siam). It has a slim body with long legs and a long neck and nose. Its fur is extremely short and its eyes are bright blue. Siamese cats usually have chocolate-brown, creamy or whitish-grey coats with darker 'points' (ears, nose and tail).

Character:	Noisy, demanding
Activity:	High
Intelligence:	High
Special needs:	Lots of attention (they love to be around people) and exercise

PERSIAN

The Persian was first brought to Europe from Iran (formerly known as Persia) by traders, although its exact origin is unknown. It has a compact body, short legs and a bushy tail. Its fur is long, thick and very soft, and comes in a number of colours. Its rounded face and short nose tend to make the Persian look grumpy.

Character:	Gentle, friendly
Activity:	Low
Intelligence:	Medium
Special needs:	Lots of grooming

MIXED-BREEDS

Most pet cats are usually mixed-breeds – a blend of several different breeds. Their appearance varies enormously, though they often have short hair. They are identified by the colour or pattern of their coat.

Tabby .... Dark stripes on body; rings round legs and tail. Various colours, including brown, ginger and shades of grey.

Tortoiseshell .... Blotches and speckles all over. Either ginger and black, or blue-grey and cream.

Tricolour/Calico .... Tortoiseshell and white.

Colourpoint .... Ears, nose, paws and tail are all darker than rest of the body.

Solid/Self-coloured .. Hairs are all one colour from root to tip.

Ticked/Agouti ..... Individual hairs have different bands of colour.

Smoked .... Fur is pale with dark tips.

Choosing a cat

When it comes to choosing a cat, you might find you're spoilt for choice. Consider all your options carefully to make sure you end up with the cat or kitten that is right for you.

Cat or kitten?

Kittens are cute and playful, but they are mischievous. They also require a lot of attention as they grow up. Adult cats are generally calmer and easier to look after than kittens. They are often a good choice if you have younger brothers or sisters, or if there are other pets at home. However, cats might find it harder to settle in.

Male or female?

It doesn't make much difference whether you choose a male or a female cat. But it is advisable to have your cat altered (see page 24). This prevents the problem of unwanted kittens. It also improves the temperament of the cat, increases its lifespan and makes it generally healthier.

Kittens and young cats are especially excited when it comes to finding out about the world outside the home. Before you let your cat out, make sure it is fully vaccinated.

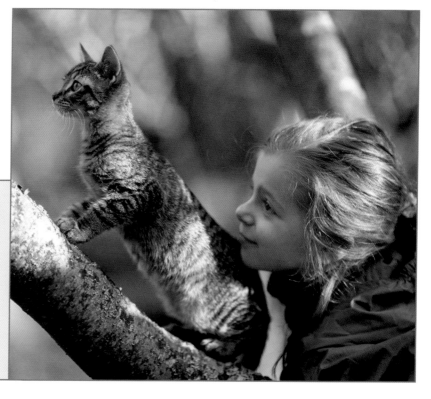

"Most cats are happy to spend some time on their own, as long as they're not neglected."

What to look for

Unless you are particularly interested in showing a cat, a mixed-breed is probably a better choice than a pedigree. Mixed-breeds are cheaper and more widely available than purebred cats. What's more, they are usually healthier, less nervous and easier to care for.

When you're buying a cat, try to find out what its parents are like. In the case of a kitten, visit the litter if you can. Watch how the mother behaves, and also look at the length of her coat. A longhaired cat will shed more hairs around the house, and will need regular grooming.

Cats love to have company, but most also enjoy time on their own. Look at the way a cat behaves before you decide to buy it.

HEALTHY SIGNS
A good choice of cat will have:

- **clean ears and nose**
- **clear, bright eyes**
- **clean, pink gums and tongue**
- **thick, shiny fur with no trace of fleas**
- **a clean rear beneath the tail**
- **a lively, friendly temperament**
- **a keen interest in its surroundings**

BUYING A CAT

Buy a pet cat from an animal shelter or professional cat breeder. Animal shelters look after unwanted pets and normally have many different cats, including kittens. If possible, visit the shelter or breeder several times before you make up your mind. Ask questions about the cat you're interested in. Rescued cats that hiss or seem afraid may have been mistreated in the past – leave these for a more experienced cat owner to adopt. It's best not to buy cats from pet shops, where the animals are often short of space and poorly cared for. For the same reasons, avoid cats offered in newspaper adverts, or on websites, even if they are being given away and you feel sorry for them.

Cat environment

Your cat needs a safe environment in which to live. It's a good idea to have everything ready before you bring your cat or kitten home.

A COMFY BED

Pet shops sell a range of cat beds, from plastic baskets to furry igloos. Even a cardboard box can become a cosy nest if you line it with a small blanket or towel. Position the bed in a warm place, such as near a radiator, where your cat won't be disturbed while it sleeps.

Kit list

Bed

Collar and tag

Bowls for food and water

Supply of food

Litter tray and cat litter

Cat carrier

Scratching post

Toys

Brush and comb

Wash your cat's bedding regularly, and check it for fleas.

"It is your responsibility to make sure your home remains a safe place for your cat to live in."

Cats use scratching posts to sharpen their claws. Buy a post to stop your cat damaging furniture at home.

A CAT-FRIENDLY HOME

Houses can be dangerous places for cats – make sure yours is safe.

DO take special care if you live in a high flat or near busy roads. Keep doors shut and consider putting mesh on windows that are open a lot.

DO check you don't have any plants that are poisonous to cats (look on the Internet or ask your vet).

DO make sure that people in your home put away potential hazards, such as poisonous cleaning fluids, sharp knives, etc.

DON'T leave electrical cables lying about – tuck them away so your cat can't chew them and get an electric shock.

DON'T let people in your home turn on the washing machine without checking your cat hasn't climbed inside.

DON'T leave human food uncovered on tables or units – your cat could jump up and eat it, which is unhealthy.

DON'T let people in your home display a precious object, such as a favourite vase, where your cat can jump up and accidentally knock it off.

CAT FLAP

Cats love exploring outside, where they can get some exercise and go to the toilet. Ask if a cat flap can be fitted in a door. There are many different types available. Then your cat can use it to pop in and out when it wants. Tape or prop the cat flap open to start with to encourage your cat to use it.

Welcome home

Moving into a new home can cause a cat distress. These tips will help you to comfort and protect your cat so that it settles in happily.

On the move

Cats don't enjoy travelling, so they need special care. Buy or borrow a cat carrier that's large enough for your cat to stand up in. Cover the base with kitchen towel, a cloth or newspaper. Don't feed your cat before the journey in case it is sick, but do take something for it to eat and drink, especially if you're going a long way.

Your cat may be wary of the carrier. Stroke your cat and coax it gently with a toy.

Settling in

For the first few days, keep your cat in a quiet room with the windows closed. Make sure it has plenty of food and water, a snug place to sleep, away from draughts, and a litter tray (see right). The cat will probably be nervous, so don't disturb it too much. Then you can allow it to explore the rest of your home. Introduce your cat to other pets and people gradually, being careful not to make sudden movements or loud noises.

"You can use a strong cardboard box as a cat carrier. Make several square holes in the top and sides to let in plenty of fresh air."

14

Toilet training

Even if you have a garden, a young kitten will need to be toilet trained. Put a litter tray on the floor in a corner of your house where it is out of the way. Then fill it with cat litter so that the kitten can scratch around. Take your kitten to the tray as soon as you first bring it home. You may also need to carry it there after meals and when it wakes up, until it learns to go by itself. Clean out the tray every 1 or 2 days, placing the contents in a separate dustbin sack. Always wear rubber gloves to do this, and wash your hands afterwards.

Cats are very clean animals by nature – they usually scrape soil or litter over their droppings to hide them.

CHOOSING A NAME

Your cat can have a human name or it might suit a more unusual one – it's up to you to decide. Some people name their cat after a place, cartoon character, celebrity, a food or even a make of car. When you have chosen a name, keep repeating it slowly and gently to your cat. Eventually your cat will learn to recognise the sound.

Cat identity collar

Buy a collar with an identity (ID) tag before you let your cat outside your home. Don't forget: you shouldn't let a kitten out until it is around 12 months old and it has been vaccinated. The ID collar will help to identify your cat if it goes missing. Include your name and telephone number – and keep the details up to date! Check the collar regularly to make sure it fits correctly.

Feeding your cat

Cats need a healthy diet of suitable food. They are carnivores (meat eaters) and like to hunt as they would in the wild. But they should eat prepared pet food.

THE RIGHT FOOD

You will find a wide range of cat foods at pet shops and supermarkets. Most of these contain everything your cat needs, including essential vitamins – look for the words 'Complete' and 'Balanced'. If you have a kitten, buy special kitten food – kittens need more protein and fat than adult cats.

DO read the instructions on the tin or packet carefully.

DO vary the kind of food you give your cat – look for different flavours and types.

DO occasionally offer some boneless fish or fresh meat, but make any changes to your cat's diet gradual.

DON'T give your cat sugary, salty or spicy foods.

DON'T give your cat lots of milk – this can cause stomach upsets, so only offer it as a special treat.

DON'T give your cat chicken bones – it might choke on the small pieces.

If your cat is alone all day, try leaving it some dried food which won't go off or attract flies. Dried food can also help to clean your cat's teeth.

WATER

Cats don't drink huge amounts of water, but it's important that they always have some available. Leave a bowl on the floor near where your cat is fed, and make sure you change the water daily. Cats that eat dried food need to drink more, because they get less liquid from their food.

MEALTIMES

Cats prefer to snack rather than have big meals, so give your cat small amounts of food regularly according to its appetite (see the table below left). Try to feed it at the same times and in the same place each day. Give your cat its own bowl and wash it out after every meal.

Age of cat	No. of daily meals
8 weeks	6
3 months	5
4 months	4
5 months	3
6+ months	2

Cats like to be left alone when they eat. Feed them in a quiet place, away from their bed and their litter tray.

HELPING THEMSELVES

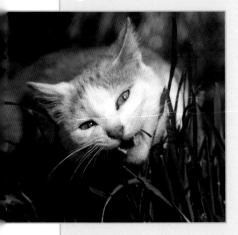

Pet cats eat grass to help their digestion. You may also see them stalking through gardens in search of mice and other small animals. Even well-fed pets hunt, although they might not eat their victims.

FAT CAT

It's unhealthy for your cat to be too fat. If you are worried yours is overweight, ask your vet for advice. You might be overfeeding your cat, or perhaps it is visiting your neighbours for extra treats! Lack of exercise could also be a problem, so make sure your cat has room to run around and explore.

Cat behaviour

Cats have their own daily routine and favourite activities. You can learn a lot about the behaviour of your cat by watching it go about its business.

Work, rest and play

Cats enjoy their sleep – they doze in cosy places for much of the day. In the wild they are mostly nocturnal (active at night). Pet cats, too, are often up and about during the night. This is usually when they wander around to inspect and protect their home territory. They may be aggressive towards other cats that come near, hissing and spitting to warn them off.

Curious cats

Cats always like to know what is going on around them. They love to perch somewhere with a good view, such as a windowsill, chair or the roof of a parked car. Many cats sit for hours in front of the television! Even when a cat appears to be dozing, it is actually still alert and stays aware of its surroundings. Its sharp senses mean it can detect the slightest sound or movement and is ready to wake up in an instant.

From the top of this wood pile, this cat has a great view of its surroundings. It is less likely to be taken by surprise.

Cat talk

The most common cat sounds are 'purring' and 'miaowing'. Purring is a constant humming noise, produced when the cat's voicebox vibrates with breathing. It is usually a sign that the cat is happy, but sometimes cats purr if they're afraid or in pain. Miaowing is a more demanding noise – your cat might miaow when it's hungry or just wants attention. Hissing and growling are sounds of anger or fear.

A cat hisses at a rival to warn it away from its territory. If that doesn't work, they may fight.

BODY LANGUAGE

Cats communicate through posture as well as sound. Watch your cat for signs of how it is feeling.

An excited cat

Eyes: wide open
Ears: point forwards
Body: back may be arched
Tail: points upwards, sways gently
Noise: chirruping or purring

A contented cat

Eyes: shut or half-shut
Ears: relaxed
Body: may roll on back or press its paws to the ground
Tail: relaxed, may sway gently
Noise: purring

An angry cat

Eyes: wide, with narrow pupils
Ears: flattened backwards
Body: tense, fur stands on end
Tail: lashes or twitches
Noise: hissing, spitting or growling

A frightened cat

Eyes: wide, with enlarged pupils
Ears: stick out to side
Body: tense, may slink down low
Tail: upright with puffed-up fur, or hanging between legs
Noise: squealing, growling or purring

Cat care

Cats are playful animals that usually enjoy human company. Playing is good exercise for your cat, as well as being great fun for both of you.

Playtime

Cats play to practise their hunting skills and also to keep fit. They may leap and pounce on anything that moves! You should play with your cat every day to stop it getting bored. All sorts of toys are available in pet shops, but many of the things cats play with cost next to nothing. Woollen balls, corks, feathers and empty toilet rolls are all fun to tap and chase. Always watch your cat playing with objects and other toys. Small pieces of string, for example, can be easily swallowed.

Cats are equally as happy with catnip-filled toys (left) as they are with simple toys, such as string.

Going on holiday

When you go away, it is better to leave your cat behind. Arrange for a neighbour or friend to feed it. If possible, they should visit twice a day. Alternatively, you could find a cattery or employ a professional cat sitter. You can find details in local newspapers, at your vet or on cat websites.

CATS LIKE:

- being stroked, gently scratched, and tickled under the chin

- cuddling on your lap – but only when they are in the mood

- being talked to softly in a soothing voice

- feeling in control

CATS DON'T LIKE:

- being forced to do things

- being teased – this will make them bad-tempered and frightened of people

- being hit or shouted at – this will make them nervous and less obedient in the future

- sudden moves or loud noises

HOW TO HOLD A CAT

There is a correct way to pick up a cat. Reach underneath the cat and hold its chest with one hand. Then use your other hand to scoop up its back legs. Cradle the cat in your arms so that it feels comfortable. Watch out for the cat's claws, and don't pick it up if it is in an aggressive mood.

PEACE AND QUIET

Remember that cats enjoy being on their own sometimes. If your cat is asleep, don't wake it up to play games. Cats need more sleep than we do, especially when they are young.

Healthy cats

Pet cats depend on their owners for simple healthcare, such as brushing and giving medicine. Vets look after more serious problems, such as cat flu.

KEEPING CLEAN

Cats keep themselves clean by licking with their tongue. It is rough which helps remove dirt and loose hair from its fur. The hair collects in its stomach and occasionally the cat has to cough it up as a furball. If you see your cat coughing, this is probably what is happening.

A mother cat grooms her kitten. A kitten has to learn how to clean itself by copying its mother.

GROOMING

Although cats groom themselves, you should still brush your cat once a week with a soft brush. Longhaired cats need to be groomed once a day. Brushing removes loose hair, dirt and dead skin. It also helps to keep the cat's coat shiny. Always brush in the direction of the cat's fur, from neck to tail – be extra careful around the head and tummy. As you go, stop regularly to remove hair from the brush.

"Visit the vet when you first get a cat
or kitten, to check that it's healthy
and up-to-date with its jabs."

SIGNS YOUR CAT
MAY BE UNWELL

- **cloudy or weepy eyes**

- **itchy or sticky ears**

- **runny nose**

- **bad breath**

- **dull, dried-out fur**

- **sneezing or persistent coughing**

- **vomiting or upset stomach**

- **appetite loss or weight loss**

- **lack of interest in surroundings**

- **constant miaowing**

VISITING THE VET

If you are worried about your cat, call the vet to ask for advice – you may need to take it to the surgery. Even a healthy cat should go for a check-up once a year. Young kittens need to have vaccinations against serious cat diseases, such as cat flu and feline leukaemia. These injections must be renewed yearly with booster jabs.

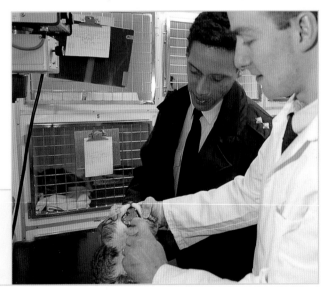

Regular health checks at the vet will ensure that your cat stays in good health.

FLEAS AND WORMS

Even the cleanest cats catch fleas, which make them itch. Buy some anti-flea powder from a pet shop and follow the directions carefully. Another problem that cats can suffer from are worms that live inside their bodies. You should give your cat an anti-worm treatment every six months or as directed by your vet.

Having kittens

Female cats are some of the best mothers in the animal world – they take great care of their young. Nevertheless, most experts recommend that you shouldn't let your cat have kittens.

Altering

If everyone let their cats breed, the world's cat population would get out of control. Already, thousands of kittens end up as strays, in shelters because they are abandoned, or dead. That's why people are strongly advised to have their pets altered (neutered or spayed). Altering is a simple operation, performed by a vet, to remove part of the cat's reproductive system and prevent it from breeding.

BE RESPONSIBLE

Think before you decide against altering (neutering or spaying):

- Cats that aren't neutered are more aggressive, restless and likely to run away.

- Your cat could escape and find a mate at any time – not just when you want it to.

- Caring for a mother cat and her young is expensive and a big responsibility.

- Cats have several kittens at once – good homes need to be found for all of them.

Kittens are born blind. They are totally dependent on their mother and her owner. It is best to leave cat breeding to the experts.

Pregnancy and birth

The average cat's pregnancy lasts for approximately nine weeks. During this time, she will need extra nutrition – if you think your cat is pregnant, ask your vet for advice.

Newborn young

At birth, kittens' eyes are sealed and they can hardly hear. But they use their noses to locate their mother's milk. They suckle for up to eight hours a day and are totally dependent on their mother for warmth and protection.

Leaving mum

Kittens' eyes open within 7–12 days. They can crawl short distances by about two weeks of age and begin to explore further at about four weeks. At first kittens are clumsy and have shaky feet, but their confidence soon grows as they start to run and play with their littermates. Kittens should not be taken away from their mother until they are at least eight weeks old.

"An 11-year-old cat is the human equivalent of 60 years old."

Kittens feed on their mother's milk. Kittens start to eat solid food when they are 6–8 weeks old.

CAT FACTS

Pregnancy	9 weeks
Possible litters per year	2–3
Average kittens per litter	3–6
Eats solid food (weaned)	6–8 weeks
Ready for new home	8–12 weeks
First jabs	8–12 weeks
Altering	5–6 months
Fully grown	8–10 months
Average lifespan	12–15 years

Wild cats

Your pet cat is closely related to lions, tigers and other big cats. Although cats vary in colour, shape and size, they often behave in similar ways.

Meet the family

The scientific name for the cat family is *Felidae.* The family includes 37 species – the domestic cat and 36 different wild cats. Wild cats are found all over the world, except in Australia where the only felines are domestic cats introduced by humans. Cats live in many different habitats, from snowy mountains to rainforests, marshes, grasslands and hot deserts.

LARGEST, SMALLEST, FASTEST!

Largest cat
Siberian Tiger (Russia)
Up to 2.8 m long/300 kg in weight

Smallest cat
Rusty-Spotted Cat (India)
About 40 cm long/1–2 kg in weight

Fastest cat
Cheetah (Africa)
Over 96 km/h (can do 0–90 km/h in 3 secs)

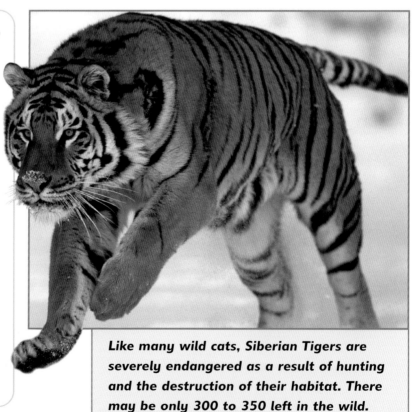

Like many wild cats, Siberian Tigers are severely endangered as a result of hunting and the destruction of their habitat. There may be only 300 to 350 left in the wild.

Natural hunters

Wild cats are
predators – they hunt
other animals, or
prey, for food. Big
cats, such as lions,
use their strong paws
and sharp claws to
tackle large prey,
including wildebeest
and antelope. Smaller
species, such as the
caracal, eat a variety of prey including rodents,
lizards and birds. All cats have pointed front
teeth designed for cutting flesh. Cats' bodies are
athletic, muscular and flexible, which enables
them to sprint, leap and climb when chasing
prey. Some cats, including the serval, even swim.

SUPER SENSES

Cats have superb senses of hearing, smell and
sight to locate prey. They can hear sounds
four or five times further away than humans
can. Have you noticed how cats' eyes glow in
a torch beam or camera flash? The ghostly
effect is caused by a special layer inside their
eyes. This produces a brighter image to help
them see better at night.

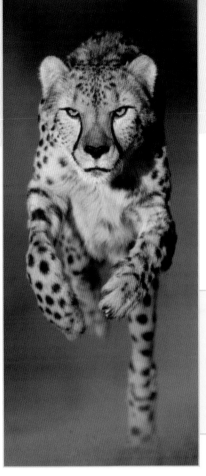

Camouflaged cats

Many wild cats have spots
or stripes. These break up
the cats' outline so that
they blend in
with their
surroundings.
Pet cats tend
to have
brighter coats
than wild cats
because camouflage is not
so important to them.

*Cheetahs'
spots match
the shades
of light and
dark in long
grass.*

*This Iberian Lynx looks
similar to some domestic
cats. It has a sandy-grey
body and looks like a large,
pale tabby.*

Losing a pet

Sadly, the typical lifespan of pet cats is about five times shorter than ours. Coming to terms with losing your cat, however it happens, can be very difficult.

FINDING A LOST CAT

Cats' curious natures sometimes cause them to wander off. Do your best to make your house and garden secure, and always encourage your cat to come back to you when it goes outside. If your cat does disappear for longer than normal, ask an adult that you know to help you find it.

- Search your neighbourhood, calling your cat's name.

- Ask your friends and neighbours if they've seen your cat.

- Check nearby roads in case there has been an accident.

- Ask if you can put up notices in local shops and at the vet's.

- Check with animal shelters near your home. Give them details and a photo of your missing cat.

Accidents and illness

You must do everything you can to stop your cat becoming ill or having an accident. But cats are independent and you can't watch them all the time. If your cat is involved in an accident or becomes ill you should take it to your vet as soon as possible. He or she will be able to assess your cat's condition and discuss the next step with you.

Loss of a friend

If your cat dies suddenly, for example as the result of an accident, the first feeling you will experience is shock; you might not feel anything at all or you might feel very emotional. If your cat dies of old age, it will be less of a shock. But this won't make your feelings easier to deal with. Talk to people around you that you trust. Tell them about what happened and about how you're feeling.

"I felt lonely when Tinker died. I didn't want to forget her so I put her picture in a frame by my bed."

Some people bury their pets in special cemeteries. Others plant trees or flowers to remember their cat by.

Act of remembrance

It is upsetting, but try not to mourn the loss of your cat for too long. Instead, celebrate the good times that you had together. You could make a scrapbook of photographs and drawings, or even write a story or poem about your cat. Many people continue to mark the birthday of their cat, even after its death, in a special way.

Saying goodbye

If you've taken good care of your cat, you mustn't blame yourself when it dies – all animals have to die eventually. But there isn't always an easy way to say goodbye. Take time to consider how you and others are feeling. You might have a younger brother or sister that is more upset than you.

AFTER THE DEATH OF A CAT

DON'T rush into buying a new cat. Also, don't accept a new cat from a friend or relative. You need to take time to consider all your options.

DON'T try to replace your cat with one that is exactly the same. Make your decision based on the animal's own characteristics.

DO think about any surviving pets you may have. For example, a dog may not get on so well with a new cat.

DO check how the rest of your family feel. Even if you're coping okay, they might not be – especially if you have younger brothers or sisters.

Glossary

Altering: The neutering or spaying of an animal.

Booster jab: A vaccination that renews the effect of a previous one.

Breed: A group of animals within the same species, whose characteristics are passed down from generation to generation. Also means to mate and have offspring, or to organise the reproduction of breeds.

Carnivore: A meat-eating animal.

Catnip: A herb that makes cats playful and relaxed.

Disease: A serious illness; bad health.

Distress: Pain, disturbance or discomfort usually caused by bad care.

Domestication: The taming of animals to keep them as pets or farm animals.

Endangered species: A species whose numbers are becoming so low it is threatened with extinction.

Habitat: The place where a plant or animal lives, for example a forest.

Medieval: A period of history in Europe from about 400 CE to about 1500.

Mixed-breed: A cat whose parents are from two or more different breeds.

Mummification: A process by which dead bodies are preserved. It was common in Ancient Egypt.

Neuter or spay: To operate on an animal so it can't have babies.

Pedigree: A pure breed of domestic animal, such as a Siamese cat.

Protein: One of the major food groups.

Species: A group of animals, such as tigers, within the cat family. Species have characteristics in common, distinct from other animals, and can reproduce together.

Vaccination: A medical treatment to prevent a particular disease, often given in the form of an injection. Also called a jab.

Weaning: To feed gradually on solid food instead of milk.

Worms: Parasites that live inside an animal's digestive system.

Websites

If you want to learn more about cats, get more advice, or become involved in animal welfare, there are several helpful organisations you can contact. Your local pet shop or vet's surgery can provide information about groups in your area. The Internet is also a good place to look. Some useful websites are listed here.

www.cats.org.uk
Cats Protection is the oldest and largest charity dedicated to cats in the UK. It rescues abandoned or vulnerable cats and rehomes them. It also provides treatment for cats and campaigns for better cat welfare. The charity has a network of 30 shelters around the UK and finds new homes for around 60,000 cats every year.

www.fabcats.org
The Feline Advisory Bureau (FAB) was established in 1958, to encourage the development of veterinary care for cats. Today, the charity not only funds veterinary research and training programmes, but also sets standards for boarding catteries. It provides advice for cat owners on all aspects of cat care, and organises regular conferences and open days throughout the UK.

www.cfainc.org
The Cat Fanciers Association (CFA) is the world's largest registry of pedigree cats and is based in the USA. Its website has a wide range of information on cat breeds and colours, cat shows and cat care.

More general information on the care, health and welfare of cats and other pets is available from a number of organisations. These include:

www.rspca.co.uk
The Royal Society for the Prevention of Cruelty to Animals (RSPCA) website has links to RSPCA websites throughout the world. It is full of information about animal adoption, news, care, training and education.

www.pdsa.org.uk
The People's Dispensary for Sick Animals (PDSA) is a charity that provides free vet services for pet owners without means. It runs a Pet Protection Club for young people that holds animal welfare events and produces a magazine with animal facts and figures, quizzes and games.

www.catchat.org/adoption/index.html
An internet-based resource providing cat care advice and a comprehensive list of UK cat shelters, with a clickable map.

www.catsofaustralia.com
This website for Cats of Australia features information about breeds and online boarding catteries, cat stories and news articles.

Every effort has been made by the Publishers to ensure that these websites contain no inappropriate or offensive material. However, because of the nature of the Internet, it is impossible to guarantee that the contents of these sites will not be altered. We strongly advise that Internet access is supervised by a responsible adult.

Index